On Monday we went
to the stores.
We got some bread.

1

On Tuesday we went
to the zoo.
We saw the animals.

On Wednesday we went
to the movies.
We saw a movie.

On Thursday we went
to the park.
We played on the swings.

On Friday we went
to the beach.
We played in the water.

On Saturday we went
to the airport.
We saw the planes.

On Sunday we went
to the hospital.
We saw our sick friend.

The next day we went
back to school.